The Heart Masters

For school children aged 5 to 8

A programme for the promotion of emotional intelligence and resilience

'The only way to have a friend is to be one.' (Ralph Waldo Emerson, 1841)

Glenda Johnston, Carol Guthrie, Andrew Fuller and Bob Bellhouse.

Lucky Duck is more than a publishing house and training agency. George Robinson and Barbara Maines founded the company in the 1980s when they worked together as a head and psychologist developing innovative strategies to support challenging students.

They have an international reputation for their work on bullying, self-esteem, emotional literacy and many other subjects of interest to the world of education.

George and Barbara have set up a regular news-spot on the website. Twice yearly these items will be printed as a newsletter. If you would like to go on the mailing list to receive this then please contact us:

Lucky Duck Publishing Ltd, 3 Thorndale Mews, Clifton, Bristol, BS8 2HX, UK

Phone: 0044 (0)117 973 2881   e-mail newsletter@luckyduck.co.uk

Fax: 044 (0)117 973 1707   website www.luckyduck.co.uk

ISBN: 1 904 315 08 9

Published by Lucky Duck Publishing Ltd. 3 Thorndale Mews, Clifton, Bristol BS8 2HX, UK

www.luckyduck.co.uk

Commissioning Editor: George Robinson
Designer: Helen Weller
Illustrator: Philippa Drakeford

Printed in the UK by Antony Rowe Limited

First published by:

GN & EJ Ridgeway
with ISBN: 0 957 767 07 2

Original trialing of the programme: Judy Kelly and Ngaro Ormsby

Contents

How to use the CD-ROM

The CD-ROM contains PDF files, labelled 'Worksheets.pdf' which contain the worksheets for each activity in this resource. You will need Acrobat Reader version 3 or higher to view and print these resources.

The document is set up to print to A4 but you can enlarge the pages to A3 by increasing the output percentage at the point of printing using the page set-up settings for your printer.

To photocopy the worksheets directly from this book, set your photocopier to enlarge by 125% and align the edge of the page to be copied against the leading edge of the the copier glass (usually indicated by an arrow).

Introduction and Rationale

Emotional intelligence requires the skills of reading the emotions of others accurately, knowing your own emotions and being able to calm or regulate your own feelings. Emotional intelligence is a critical factor in career and educational success.

Resilience is the happy knack of bungee jumping through the pitfalls of life. Three critical factors that promote resilience are:

▸ feeling loved by your family
▸ peer connectedness
▸ fitting in at school.

Together the habits and skills of emotional intelligence and resilience can be taught and developed in young people. Not only do they provide a powerful way of protecting young people against suicide, violence and substance abuse, they also promote the skills that lead to success in social and organisational settings.

This programme is designed to develop the key aspects of resilience and emotional intelligence:

▸ the ability to read and take into consideration the feelings of others
▸ an awareness of our own feelings
▸ the ability to regulate or calm our feelings
▸ a sense of connectedness and belonging.

How to Use this Book

Key learning areas

The Heart Masters has been developed for lower primary aged children (5 to 8 years). The key learning areas for this unit are:

▸ Health
▸ Language
    - Speaking and listening
    - Reading
    - Writing
▸ Drama
▸ Visual Arts
▸ Mathematics

Programme delivery and duration

It is recommended that this unit be delivered in the first term of the school year as many of the experiences and activities are designed to assist students to settle into the class and set the scene to create a safe the supportive learning environment.

The programme is divided into eight organising themes. A range of key learning areas are included within each theme.

The programme has a strong language focus and it is recommended that many of the language based activities are delivered during timetabled language blocks. This will reduce the time taken to deliver the unit, as well as leave time within the term to cover other important topics and concepts. It is envisaged that the unit, if included within normal language blocks, would run for approximately five to eight weeks.

To assist programme planning, the following symbols indicate activities that have a language focus.

 Writing

Reading

 Speaking and listening

The use of drama and role-play

One of the major teaching and learning strategies used in this unit is drama and role-play. Inclusion of these strategies is to ensure students:

▸ relate understandings and concepts as much as possible to their personal experience
▸ are provided with opportunities to rehearse repertoire and skills.

The confidence and skill of children to successfully undertake drama and role-play activities will depend on age and previous experience.

If you feel students are inexperienced, ensure that you model the scenarios and role-plays with other staff, older students or more confident students. Then provide students with opportunities to copy and explore the role-plays for themselves.

Programme Outline and Organising Themes

Theme One: Welcome!

Week one introduces the themes of belonging and joining in, and sets the scene for creating an inclusive and supportive classroom environment. Being welcomed and making others feel welcome is an important start to students gaining confidence and feeling a sense of belonging in a group. Students practise ways of making people feel welcome, make a welcome sign for the classroom, and go to the zoo to find out why some people find it difficult to welcome people or belong to a group.

Theme Two: Rules Rules Rules

Through games and real life scenarios children are introduced to the concept of rules and why they are needed. The children are also involved in the development of rules that will help to create a happy and supportive learning environment. The children make posters to reinforce concepts and are rewarded for appropriate behaviour.

Theme Three: I'm Special, You're Special

This week focuses on getting to know each other. Similarities and differences between students in the class are identified through a range of language and mathematics activities. Names and characteristics of students are celebrated and a special chart to remember birthdays is created.

Theme Four: Learning About Feelings

During week four the children explore feelings. Through movement and drama they are provided with opportunities to identify their own feelings and the feelings of others. They also discuss and rehearse helping strategies they can use when their family or friends are feeling down. They make a range of marvellous masks to reinforce concepts. These masks can also be used to assist children experiencing difficult emotions to talk about how they feel.

Theme Five: Cool, Calm and In Control

Movement, drama and creative visualisation are used to demonstrate the concepts of being calm and in control. The children also explore how difficult it is to solve problems when their bodies won't let their heads work. Calming strategies are taught and practised and a poster is made as a prompt for the children to use when they are feeling anxious.

Theme Six: Mistakes and Muck-ups

In 'Mistakes and Muck-ups' children explore what might go wrong to spoil a good time. Children also learn that they can fix and get over mistakes and muck-ups. 'It's a mucked-up moment, but I can fix it' is a slogan taught to the children to assist them to think positively about difficult situations they may face. Solutions for a range of age related problems are explored as are the problems of some of our favourite nursery rhyme characters.

Theme Seven: Bunji

During week six the children are introduced to Bunji, a rather shy character from another land that has come to join the class. The children have a lot to teach Bunji and Bunji has a lot to teach the children. The arrival of Bunji puts all of the children's new skills into action as they prepare to welcome him and help him settle into his new school. With the help of the children, Bunji is transformed into a bouncy, resilient and fun loving character that learns that it is better to face problems than to avoid them.

Theme Eight: Party Time!

By now the children have a lot to celebrate. They have worked hard all term and have demonstrated what a caring and friendly class they are. A party is certainly in order but a good party needs to be planned and everyone has to do their bit. Party preparations help to build a sense of belonging and teamwork as everyone works together for a common purpose.

Not only are party preparations conducted but a 'Happy Party Poster' is made to ensure everyone has a good time.

Theme **1**

Welcome

Theme 1 introduces the themes of belonging and joining in, and sets the scene for creating an inclusive and supportive classroom environment. Being welcomed and making others feel welcome is an important start to students gaining confidence and feeling a sense of belonging in a group. Students practise ways of making people feel welcome, make a welcome sign for the classroom, and go to the zoo to find out why some people find it difficult to welcome people or belong to a group.

Activity 1: Welcome To Our Class

Purpose

▶ to introduce the themes of joining in and belonging
▶ to discuss, model and rehearse a range of welcoming strategies that children can use in everyday situations.

Resources

▶ Worksheet 1: 'Welcome'
▶ a puppet
▶ two pieces of A3 paper, one headed 'Ways to make people feel welcome', the other headed, 'Why might people feel unwelcome'.(See example)
▶ some paper and crayons.

Ways to make people feel WELCOME	Why people might feel UNWELCOME
We can SMILE	Run away
We can SHAKE HANDS	Say hurtful things
We can say, 'HELLO'	Stare at someone
We can say, 'JOIN US'	Stay apart.
We can say, 'SHARE OUR TOYS'	Hit someone
We can put up A WELCOME SIGN	Say rude words

Procedure

1. Introduce the class to the idea of making people feel welcome by using a puppet that introduces itself to the class and asks if it can join in.
2. As responses from the students are received make the puppet react accordingly. For example, after a positive response show how happy the puppet is or if a student provides a negative response show emotions of sadness.

3. Following interactions between the puppet and the students discuss how the puppet feels and if the puppet feels welcome or unwelcome.
4. Discuss what 'welcome' means. For example, 'Glad to see you.' 'Come in here.' 'Join our game.' 'We like you being here'.
5. Make a class poster.
6. Discuss phrases and actions that will make people feel welcome and unwelcome. Write the phrases and actions onto prepared A3 paper.
7. Ask students to enact small role-plays in which they practise welcoming responses. Alternatively, provide students with puppets to practise responses.
8. Students draw and write about how they would like to be treated if they were new to a place or wanted to participate in the activities with others.

Student work could be made into a book or frieze.

Extension Activities

▶ Give students Worksheet 1: 'Welcome' for homework. Students and families describe the welcoming gestures they use to welcome people to their homes.

▶ Interview the head or other class teachers about how they welcome people.

▶ Students find out how to say 'Welcome' in other languages. Make a poster and nominate a different way of saying welcome each week. 'Welcome', 'Bongiorno', 'Bonjour 'etc.

Discuss safety issues in relation to Stranger Danger.

Worksheet 1: Welcome

Name: _____

Please fill this homework sheet in for your child.

Our special way of saying welcome is: _____

At our house we welcome people by:

1. _____

2. _____

3. _____

4. _____

5. _____

6. _____

Draw a picture of how we
welcome other people.

Activity 2: A Very Special Welcome Sign

Purpose
▸ to reinforce and extend concepts introduced in activity one.
▸ to strengthen the concept of being in an inclusive, friendly and welcoming class.

Resources
▸ a camera
▸ some A3 paper.

Procedure
1. Children discuss the homework sheets completed at home.
2. Ask what sort of special things we can do to welcome people to our classroom. Choose some gestures to incorporate into your daily routine.
3. Inform the class that they are going to make a special welcome sign for the classroom door. Tell them that you will be using photographs and words that will show visitors what a friendly and caring class they are.
4. Discuss photographs and words that should be included.
5. Take a number of photographs of the children in poses that reflect the above, for example, the whole class with their arms around the shoulders of others and waving.

Extension Activities
▸ Students research other places that have welcome signs (country towns, hospitals, sports grounds etc.).

Activity 3: Visitors Welcome

Purpose
▸ to explore a range of friendly gestures
▸ to demonstrate that some people find it difficult to be friendly
▸ to promote tolerance of those that experience difficulty.

Resources

▸ the 'Visitors Welcome' story
▸ a Stop signal.

Procedure

1. Explain to the children that they are going to visit the zoo to see if the animals there are being friendly. Also tell them that they will have to pretend they are animals so that the zoo animals do not notice them.
2. Divide the class into groups. Nominate groups to represent the following animals:

Hyena
Howling

Elephants
Trumpeting

Monkeys
Chattering

Bandicoots
Squeaking

Parrots
Squawking

Lions
Roaring

3. Instruct each group to practise the animal noise of their animal.
4. Tell them that every time the name of their animal is mentioned they have to make the noise.
5. Establish a Stop signal to stop the animal noises being made.
6. Ask students to practise their animal noises.
7. Read the 'Visitors Welcome' story.
8. Read the story a second time. This time ask the students not to make the animal noises.

9. Whenever you see this symbol [**?**] stop reading and ask the children if this is a friendly or unfriendly gesture. This could be done showing happy or sad faces or thumbs up and thumbs down to show how the visitor might feel. Alternatively, use the following questions with students who have more advanced language skills.

> Would this make you feel welcome?
> If yes, why? If no, why not?
> Why do you think the animal finds if hard to be friendly?
> Does the animal have a problem?
> Can the problem be fixed?

10. At the end of the story ask how Aunt Ettie and the child show they are friendly.

Extension Activities

▶ Use the 'Visitors Welcome' story as a shared reading or individual reading text.

▶ Groups of students act out scenes from Visitors Welcome or make up their own scenes.

▶ Students draw or write about how they would make a new child, a person from the moon, a giant, or anyone else, welcome in their class. What would they need?

Visitors Welcome

Welcome! My name is Gertie. Aunt Ettie and I went to the zoo to see the animals.

The sign at the zoo said, 'Visitors Welcome', so I said to my Aunt Ettie, 'Does that mean we can go in?

She said, 'Yes, but after we pay!' She took out her purse and went to the cashier's window to buy our tickets. She was surprised to find a very friendly monkey behind the counter.

'Glad you could come. We need all the visitors we can get.'

At a desk she saw a goat with big spectacles, counting the money. A sign on the goat's desk read, 'I am not a silly old goat, I'm a very busy goat!'

Inside the gate I thought, 'What a lot of noises!'

    Monkeys were chattering.

    Lions were roaring.

    Elephants were trumpeting.

    Hyenas were howling.

    Parrots were squawking.

Snakes were hissing.

Bandicoots were squeaking.

'Where shall we go first?', I asked Aunt Ettie.

She studied the map the friendly monkey had given her.
'This way', she said pointing towards the birds.

So off we went. As we got closer I heard some very loud
talking going on.

'Try it one more time.

Now listen.

'Pleased to meet you.

Pleased to meet you.

Polly want a cracker!

Polly want a cracker!'

squawked a young cockatoo sitting high up
in a tree.

'No I don't!', answered a rather frustrated looking parrot.

'And don't call me Polly.

My name is Richard. Got it!

How many times do I have to tell you?'

'Polly want a cracker,

Polly want a cracker',

continued the cockatoo.

As we got closer the parrot turned and looked at us.
Aunt Ettie and I stopped and started to turn away.

We thought maybe it wasn't a good time to visit
the parrots.

'Don't go,' called the parrot.

'It's lovely to speak to someone who can say more than four words. Cockatoo is only learning to talk, and I'm afraid I'm getting tired of hearing the same words over and over again. Please stay and talk to me.'

We stayed and talked to the parrot for a while. He explained that cockatoo could only speak cockatoo and that he wasn't being rude, he just hadn't learned how to speak English yet.

We thanked the parrot for spending time with us and turned to leave. As we were walking away, the cockatoo yelled.

'Pleased to eat stew.'

'By George, you've nearly got it!', shouted the parrot with surprise.

'Pleased to eat stew

Pleased to eat stew

Pleased to eat stew.'

We laughed and walked to the bandicoot enclosure.

When we got there, the place seemed empty. We looked and looked but couldn't see the bandicoots anywhere.

'Hello bandicoots'. There was no answer.

I called again.

Aunt Ettie pointed over to a mound of dry leaves near a log. We could just see a tiny little nose and whiskers poking out from under the leaves. We could also see the leaves shaking.

We called the bandicoots again but they wouldn't come out.

'Hmmm', sighed Aunt Ettie. She reached into her bag and took out a piece of bread and jam that we were going to have for lunch.

She gently placed it on the grass and said, 'Let's just watch'.

In a while two very cute little bandicoots came out from under the grass with their little noses sniffing madly. Very, very, very slowly they made their way over to the bread and started to nibble. Just then Aunt Ettie dropped her hat on the ground and the two little bandicoots ran into the bushes.

Aunt Ettie said, 'Perhaps we should leave them be?'

As we turned away a soft little voice called out, 'Thank you for coming, please come again'.

I looked back, and with a huge grin I whispered, 'Goodbye, you take care now.'

The next stop according to our map was the Hyena enclosure.

On nearing the enclosure I could hear some growling and grunting. Then suddenly the growling and grunting stopped. We got closer. When we got to the fence a very rude voice called out.

'Get Lost! We don't want the likes of you around here!'

We looked at each other with surprise.

'You heard. Get lost.... buzz off. Take a long walk on a

short pier. Keep those feet moving'.

'Who do you think you are!'

'Get Lost!'

'I beg your pardon', said Aunt Ettie in a very cross voice. 'Who do you think you are? You can't talk to people like that?'

'The King of Siam. The Queen of Sheba. The Sultan Of Brunei. Take your pick, then get lost!'.

'My word', said Aunt Ettie. 'I haven't ever been spoken to like that before'.

'If you stick around here you'd better get used to it baby, because there's more of the same coming your way'.

With that, the hyena started grunting and laughing and grunting and howling and grunting and laughing some more. He was grunting and laughing so much that he backed into a pine tree. He hit it so hard that a huge pine cone dropped out of the tree and hit him right on the head.

'Serves you right you rude beast', laughed Aunt Ettie.

We laughed all the way to the snake house.

Aunt Ettie looked at the sign on the stone wall and said, 'I don't think I want to go in there. Snakes are so slimy and cold'.

'But Aunt Ettie, I want to see the snakes. I've waited all day to see them. It will be okay. Just stand back if you're nervous'.

I took her by the hand and led her into the cold and dimly lit snake house.

'Sssssstep in here. It'sssss, sssssso good to ssssssssssee you.'

Aunt Ettie stepped back. Her hand was shaking.

I walked slowly over to the snake pit. 'How do you do?' I asked.

'Sssssssssssuper', came the reply from a large Python named Simon.

I knew his name was Simon because it said so on the sign above the pit.

'Is the ssssssssssun outssssssside warm today?', sighed Simon.

'Yessssssss. I mean, yes', I answered, 'It's a beautiful day outside. Don't you ever get to go out?'.

'No. The zoo keeper ssssssssssays I always frighten the cussssssssstomers'.

'Why do you frighten the customers?', asked Aunt Ettie.

'I don't mean to. It'sssssssss just the way I look and talk. I look and talk differently to all the other animalssss. Before I get a chance to ssssssssay, ssssssssssalutationsss (that's another way of saying hello) they run away,' cried Simon. 'I get ssssssso embarasssssssed that I don't even try to talk to people any more. I am ssssso lonely'.

I had an idea!

'Have you ever thought of starting your greeting with something other than a word that starts with 'S'?'

 'Why? What good would that do?'

'Well, think about it. Try it. Try saying, 'Hello'.

'Hello', said Simon clearly and sharply.

'Now try saying, 'Hello, great weather we're having'.

Simon drew a deep breath and said, 'Hello, great weather we're having.'

'Don't you see Simon. It's the Esses. They're what are scaring the customers'.

'Are you sssssssssssssssssssssssssure?', asked Simon.

'Sure. I'm positive. Keep the 'S' words for your friends'.

'Thank you friend', smiled Simon.

'Don't worry Simon', said Aunt Ettie, 'We will talk to the zoo keeper and see what can be done. Until then we will come and visit you each Saturday and I'll bring a hot water bottle to keep you warm'.

With that we heard a siren sound.

'You had better get going. They will lock the gates ssssssoon', said Simon.

Bye bye Simon!

We made our way to the door of the snake house. 'Goodbye', we called.

'Sssssssssssssssssseeya, I mean, bye bye!', shouted Simon.

We ran quickly out of the snake house down the path past the hyena (who was still out cold at the bottom of the tree) past the Elephants past the Lions past the Monkeys past the Bandicoots past the Parrots and through the gate before the zoo keeper locked it for the evening.

ZOO IS CLOSED

Theme (2)

Rules Rules Rules

Through games and real life scenarios children are introduced to the concept of rules and why they are needed. The children are also involved in the development of rules that will help to create a happy and supportive learning environment. The children make posters to reinforce concepts and are rewarded for appropriate behaviour.

Activity 4: Why We Have Rules

Purpose

▸ to make students aware of the need for rules and prepare them for developing their own classroom rules.

Resources

▸ a piece of A3 paper headed, 'Why we have rules'.

Procedure

1. Ask students if they know what a rule is.
2. Ask students for examples of rules. After each response, ask what the rule is for and discuss what might happen if the rule didn't exist.
3. Read the following scenarios to the students. Alternatively use the scenarios as a shared reading text. After each scenario ask:

    ▸ Are the people in the story happy? If yes, why? If not, why not?
    ▸ Is what happened fair to everyone?
    ▸ Can we make a rule to keep everyone happy and safe?

Scenario 1

Amanda, Kylie, Tran, Cory and Joshua were painting. Everyone made a very big mess. Cory had to clean up by himself. It took a very long time and he missed out on playtime.

Scenario 2

All of the children were inside the classroom. Fred was playing with a football. It went through the window. Glass went everywhere. The teacher was cross. The teacher said the children could never get the ball back and she would give it to some other children.

Scenario 3

John, Teresa and Ben were playing chase. Teresa made John be the 'chaser' every time. John was not very happy.

Scenario 4

All of the children were drawing at their tables. Phillip was leaning back on his chair. He leant back so far, his chair fell and he hit his head. He had to go to the doctor for stitches.

Scenario 5

Mario, Alex, Rebecca and Carl were having running races. Mario was running as fast as he could. He tried very, very hard but he did not win.

Alex called him a big 'sissy la la' and hurt Mario's feelings very much. Mario didn't want to go in running races again.

Scenario 6

Lisa forgot to tell her teacher she was going to the toilet. While she was out the teacher took the class to the art room. When Lisa got back, the classroom was empty. Lisa got frightened and tried to find her class. While the teacher and the rest of the children were in the art room, Lisa's teacher realised Lisa was not there. She was very worried. She sent for the headteacher and asked them to find Lisa. The head was worried too. Finally Lisa found her class and walked into the classroom. The head and the teacher were very cross with her.

4. After discussing scenarios ask students why we have rules.
5. Write responses onto your prepared, 'Why we have rules?' poster.

Activity 5: Happy Classroom Rules

Purpose

▶ to involve the children in the process of developing a list of classroom rules and consequences that will help to create a safe and supportive learning environment
▶ to demonstrate that positive behaviour will be rewarded.

Resources

▶ 'Thumbs Up' Awards.

Procedure

1. Provide students with an opportunity to recall and reflect on the previous session.
2. Ask students to make suggestions for rules that would help to make this classroom a safe and happy place.

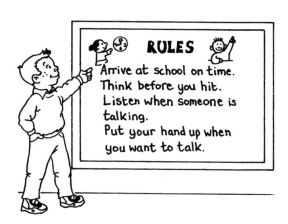

3. List suggestions on the board.
4. If children are struggling to come up with a range of realistic and appropriate rules, refer to the scenarios previously discussed.
5. Discuss what happens if rules are broken.
6. Display rules in the classroom.
7. Frequently reward positive behaviour, look for the 'good'!

Extension Activities

▶ Give each student a different rule to illustrate and make this into a class book or wall frieze.

▶ Tell the students that an imaginary student, called 'Thora'', does lots of silly things at school. Tell the students you will tell them some of the things that Thora does. Each time Thora does something that is following the rules, ask them to show you a thumbs up sign. If Thora does something that is against the school rules, show a thumbs down sign.

> For example:
>
> Thora plays in the sand pit.
>
> Thora brings her pet snake to school.
>
> Thora asks the teacher to go to the toilet.
>
> Thora pushes Charlie out of the door.
>
> Thora calls her friend a stupid idiot.

▶ Teacher starts a 'Thumbs Up' Award. Each week students who follow the rules are presented with an award.

▶ Make up music and words for singing the Rules Rap.

▶ Students find out what rules they have for their pet. They draw their pet in situations where the rules are being kept and when they are not.

▶ Make a 'Ready Ruler' for the class with ascending numbers on it - when the class gets enough Thumbs Up there is a class treat, for example, a game.

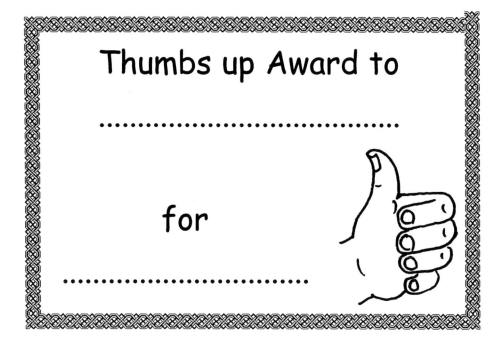

Thumbs up Award to

....

for

....

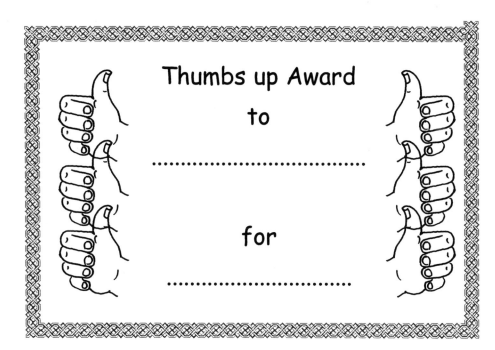

Thumbs up Award to

....

for

....

THE HEART MASTERS

Theme 3

I'm Special, You're Special

This theme focuses on getting to know each other. Similarities and differences between students in the class are identified through a range of language and mathematics activities. Names and characteristics of students are celebrated and a special chart to remember birthdays is created.

Activity 6: Special Names for Special People

Purpose

▶ to help students get to know each other
▶ to stimulate interest in other students
▶ to reinforce that everyone in the class is a special person.

Resources

▶ name card for each student. Place birth dates in large print on the back of the cards, for example, Iris, 15 July.
▶ a range of items that can be used to decorate a name card, for example, sequins, pipe cleaners, pasta, coloured pens, confetti etc.
▶ special name box.
▶ a die.

Procedure

1. Discuss:

Why are names important?

If you say someone's name, why does it make that person feel included and special?

What would it be like if people didn't have names?

2. Play the following name games:

I know

Teacher asks students to stand in a circle, close their eyes and in turn say their own name and the names of other students they can remember.

For example,

'My name is and I know...and...'.

On my right, on my left

Ask the students to sit in a circle.

Ask students to look carefully at the people to the right of them.

Ask students to close their eyes and say in order, as many names as they can remember.

Then reverse the direction and ask students to name as many other students on their left.

Guess Who

Blindfold three students and make them stand out the front.

Choose three other students to come out the front and stand one with each of the blindfolded students.

The blindfolded students must feel the faces of the other children and try and guess who they are.

The Name Box

Show students the name box; all children's names in the class are in the box.

Tell students that the names of very special and important people are in the box. Students pick a name from the name box and go back to their seat to colour and decorate around the letters.

Seat students in a circle. Each student says the name of their special person, one special thing about that person and presents them with their name card.

Ask the children if they know when their birthdays are. Go through the months of the year and ask the children to stand up when you say their birthday month. Have your register on hand to help students that do not know when their birthday is.

Extension Activities

▸ Devise a system so that student's birthdays are celebrated.
▸ Students graph how many names start with the same letter. Which are the most popular letters?
▸ Students find out the names of their sisters and brothers. How many are the same? How old are the brothers and sisters? Who has the oldest/youngest brother and sister?

Activity 7: My Name's Special and So Am I

Purpose
▸ to focus on positive characteristics of self and others
▸ to develop concepts of positive self regard.

Resources
▸ pieces of A3 paper
▸ overhead projector or bright light.

Procedure
1. Make a silhouette of each child's head and shoulders and write the name of each student on to the silhouette.
2. Discuss how everyone in the class is special.

Turn each person's name into an acrostic poem by asking the students to come up with a word or sentence that starts with each letter in their name and describes the person.

Activity 8: Same and Different Games

Purpose
▸ to stimulate interest in other students
▸ to provide an opportunity for students to share personal information
▸ to demonstrate personal similarities and differences.

Resources
▸ some mirrors
▸ a Stop signal.

Procedure

1. Discuss how people in the class are the same in some ways and different in other ways. Tell the students they are going to play games about being the same and about being different.

Stand Up

Ask all students to sit on the floor.

Ask students to stand up if they have, or do, the following:

All children who:

    have brown eyes

    walk to school

    have a mouth

    sleep in a bed

    have blonde hair

    wear a school uniform

    have black shoes

    own a bird

    have arms

    own a dog

    have freckles

    like ice cream

    have been to the beach

    like spaghetti

Find A Friend

Ask students to form a group with other people who have the same:

    colour eyes
    colour hair
    colour shoes
    colour socks

Spot the Difference

Ask three children to stand out the front– two children with the same coloured eyes, one with a different colour.

Tell the children that two people have something the same and one person has something different and ask the children to spot the difference.

Repeat with other children. Add categories, for example hair colour, ethnicity, sex, hair length and height.

Discuss

▶ how are we the same?
▶ how are we different?
▶ what would it be like if everyone was the same?

Activity 9: My Favourite Things

Purpose

- to stimulate interest in other students
- to provide an opportunity for students to share personal information
- to demonstrate personal similarities and differences.

Resources

- 'My Favourite Things' Worksheet
- a Stop signal.

Procedure

Be on the alert to identify students who do not find students to match. This may cause them to feel left out and upset. You can always find a match between yourself and the left out student. Be proactive.

1. Tell students that in the last session you looked at lots of ways that people were the same and different. Recap on some of the similarities and differences. Today you will look at how people think the same and think differently.
2. Students fill in Worksheet 2: 'My Favourite Things'.
3. Tell students that they are going to play the 'My Favourite Things Matching Game'.
4. To play the game they need to:
   > Go up to someone and say,
   > 'My favourite food is...'
   > 'What is your favourite food?'

   Tell them that when they find someone who thinks the same, they hold hands together and try to find others who also think the same.
5. Stop the activity and ask groups of children to identify their favourite food.
6. Identify students who could not find a match. Point out that it is okay to think differently and the rest of the class will respect what they think. People who think differently are special and unique.
7. Ask all the students who could not find a match to hold hands and form a separate group.
8. Do the same for the following:
   > My favourite animal is
   > My favourite drink is
   > My favourite TV programme is
   > My favourite game is
   > My favourite song is

9. Discuss the concept of respecting how other people think, for example that means we don't:

> laugh at people's ideas
> hurt people
> tease people
> call people names
> make fun of people.

Extension Activities

▸ Using pictures from magazines, each student makes a collage of the things they like.

▸ Students play a 'Guess what I like' headband game.

> Make a headband.

> Each student draws a picture of something they like, and then labels their picture.

> The teacher asks for a volunteer.

> Attach one of the labelled pictures to the headband and place on the student's head, without them seeing the picture.

> The student asks questions and tries to guess the 'favourite thing'.

> Students might then wish to guess whose 'favourite thing' it is.

▸ Play, discuss and teach 'My Favourite Things' from *The Sound Of Music*.

▸ Students draw a picture of their favourite things and show their pictures in show and tell.

Worksheet 2   Name:.....................................

My Favourite Things

My favourite food is

....

My favourite animal is

....

My favourite drink is

....

My favourite TV programme is

....

My favourite game is

....

My favourite song is

....

Activity 10: About Me, About Us

Purpose

▸ to stimulate interest in other students
▸ to provide an opportunity for students to share personal information
▸ to demonstrate personal similarities and differences.

Resources

▸ 'About Me' Worksheet (one for each student)
▸ 'Graph - Where Our Families Come From' Worksheet
  (as many as needed)
▸ 'Graph - Our Hair Colour' Worksheet (as many as needed)
▸ 'Graph - Our Eye Colour' Worksheet (as many as needed)
▸ 'Graph - Our Cars' Worksheet (as many as needed).
  (Enlarge Worksheets to A3 if necessary.)

Procedure

1. Provide students with the 'About Me' Worksheet. This Worksheet is to be completed with families. Information from this Worksheet will be used to make a series of graphs.
2. Ask students to come up and show their 'About Me' Worksheets and tell the other children about themselves.
3. Ask them to sit in pairs and go through the information on their sheets with their partners. Select students to tell the class about their partners.
4. Collect 'About Me' Worksheets to work out how many graphs you will need to prepare. For example, if you have students who have families from six different countries you will need six 'Where Our Families Come From Graphs'.
5. Ask students to place their information from the 'About Me' Worksheets onto relevant graphs (Worksheets 4-7) and discuss the findings.

Worksheet 3   About Me

This is me

My name is

....

My Phone Number

....

I live at

....

My family comes from

....

My family has a car.

Yes / No

Its colour is

....

My eyes are

....

My hair colour is

....

Worksheet 4   Where our Families Come From

Our families come from

....

Student Names	Bar Graph

....

....

....

....

....

....

....

8
7
6
5
4
3
2
1

People in our class have families that come from

....

Our Hair Colour

We have

....hair

Student Names	Bar Graph

....

....

....

....

....

....

....

....

8
7
6
5
4
3
2
1

People in our class have

....hair.

Worksheet 6   Our Eye Colour

Our eye colour is

....

Student Names	Bar Graph

.... | 8 |

.... | 7 |

.... | 6 |

.... | 5 |

.... | 4 |

.... | 3 |

.... | 2 |

.... | 1 |

People in our class have

....eyes.

Worksheet 7   Our Cars

Our cars are

....

Student Names	Bar Graph

....

....

....

....

....

....

....

....

Bar Graph
8
7
6
5
4
3
2
1

People in our class have

....car.

Theme 4

Surprised Faces

Learning About Feelings

During theme four the children explore feelings. Through movement and drama they are provided with opportunities to identify their own feelings and the feelings of others. They also discuss and rehearse helping strategies they can use when their family or friends are feeling down. They make a range of marvellous masks to reinforce concepts. These masks can also be used to talk about any difficult emotions children are experiencing.

Activity 11: Feelings

Purpose

▸ to explore different feelings people have
▸ to explore how we can tell how we and others are feeling
▸ to promote a caring and supportive classroom environment.

Resources

▸ a collection of pictures and photographs that display a range of emotions
▸ an open space for drama activities
▸ mirrors.

Procedure

1. Say to the students, 'I am feeling…today'. Go around the class asking, 'And how are you feeling today?'
2. Discuss how you can often tell how people are feeling by the way they look, the noises they make and the things they say.
3. Show students pictures and photographs and ask students:
   How the character is feeling?
   Why they might be feeling that way?
   How we can tell they are feeling that way?
   What might the character say?
   Elicit responses from looking at their faces, from the noises they make and from the way their bodies look.
4. Some students may be unfamiliar with some of the terminology used. As each feeling is explored talk about why people might feel that way and whether they like the feeling or not. Use thumbs up for describing a feeling they like and thumbs down for describing a feeling they do not like.
5. Provide students with mirrors and encourage them to make faces.
6. Take photographs of the faces students make.
7. Sit the students in a circle and ask them to close their eyes while other students make a noise that demonstrates a feeling. Students then guess what the feeling is.
8. Ask students to use all of the above to show a feeling. Take photographs.
9. Make a feelings book. Distribute photographs the teacher took, and ask students to write about the feeling they are displaying and why they feel the way they do.

Activity 12: Caring For Your Friends

Purpose

▶ to promote a caring and supportive classroom environment
▶ to provide students with helping strategies

Resources

▶ a Stop signal.

Procedure

1. Ask students what causes people to be unhappy.
2. Ask students what we can do if someone isn't happy. How can we help?
3. Brainstorm a list of responses.
4. Tell students that they can try some of the ideas out.

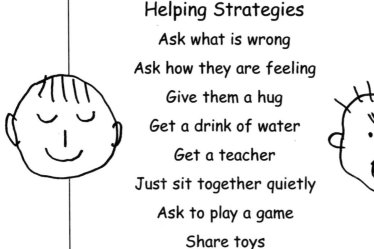

Helping Strategies

Ask what is wrong

Ask how they are feeling

Give them a hug

Get a drink of water

Get a teacher

Just sit together quietly

Ask to play a game

Share toys

Suggest ideas to help solve the problem.

5. Model the following scenarios for children:
   Scenario 1
   You are a new student and you are missing your friends from your old school.
   Scenario 2
   You have just lost your dog. You can't find it anywhere.

6. Choose students to use strategies from the list to try and make the teacher feel better.
7. Choose students to come out and replay the same scenes that the teacher modelled.
8. Ask students to find a partner. Nominate one of the above scenarios and ask children to participate in a role-play in which helping strategies are practised.
9. Discuss what you should you do if a friend does not want to be helped. Responses could include:

> Tell an adult.
>
> Just sit with them.
>
> Leave them alone and try and help them later.

Activity 13: Marvellous Masks

Purpose

▸ to provide a strategy to help students identify and express their emotions.

Resources

▸ the Marvellous Masks copied onto card (Worksheets 8A to 8F).

Procedure

1. Provide students with an opportunity to recall work previously covered on feelings and faces. Reinforce different types of feelings, how they look and feel and whether they like them or not.
2. Tell students: that you have a special surprise-you have made some special masks that they can use to show how they are feeling. They can use these masks at any time they are having feelings they would like to share. The masks will be displayed in a special place and they will need to be careful and look after the masks so that other people can use them also.

On the following Worksheets you will find a selection of masks that portray feelings. They can be copied onto coloured card, decorated and used by students to identify feelings.

These masks may also be useful in encouraging angry and upset students with a prop to identify and express their feelings. This in turn may provide you with an opportunity to implement helping strategies of your own.

Worksheet 8A Marvellous Masks - Happy

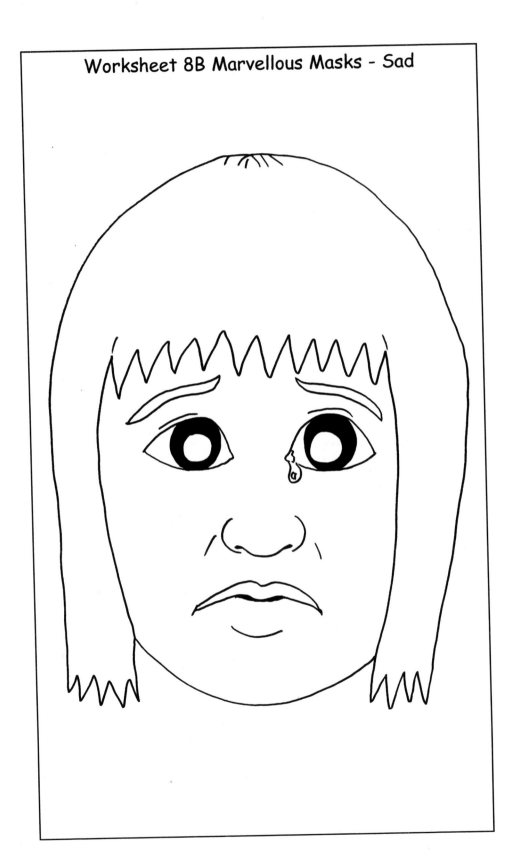

Worksheet 8D Marvellous Masks – Tired

THE HEART MASTERS

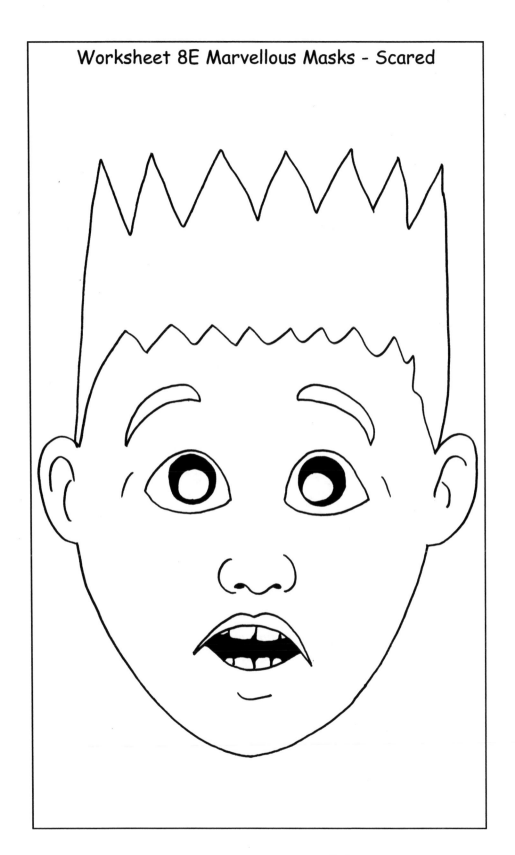

Worksheet 8F Marvellous Masks - Annoyed

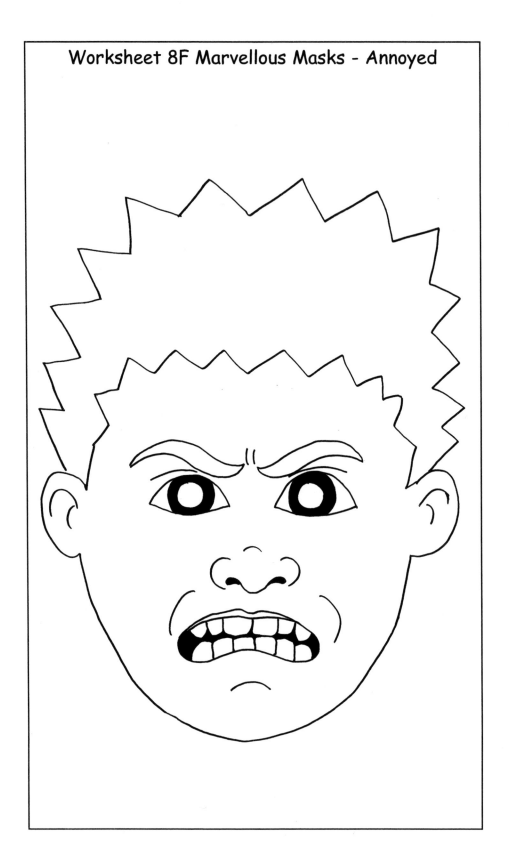

THE HEART MASTERS

What happened?

How they felt?

How they fixed it?

How they felt at the end?

Cool, Calm and In Control

Movement, drama and creative visualisation are used to demonstrate the concepts of being calm and in control. Children also explore how difficult it is to solve problems when their body won't let their head work. Calming strategies are taught and practised and a poster is made as a prompt for children to use when they are feeling anxious.

Activity 14: Calm the Waters

Purpose

▸ to explore, identify and describe the concepts of feeling calm, as well as opposite concepts such as worried, hysterical, anxious, out of control etc.

Resources

▸ an open space for drama activities
▸ a Stop signal
▸ Worksheet 9: 'Calm and Not Calm'.

Procedure

1. Ask students what the word calm means and why people may need to calm down. Listen to and discuss responses provided by students.
2. Inform students that today they are going to play a lot of games that will teach them more about what it means to be calm.
3. Instruct students that they are not to talk or touch other students. Reinforce the Stop signal that you have introduced to the class.
4. Ask students to stand up and find a place to stand in the room. Tell them that you will call out things that you want them to act out.

> Be an old lady sleeping in her rocking chair.
> Be a soldier marching along the road.
> Be a lion roaring at a hunter with a gun.
> Be a kitten lying in front of a nice warm fire.
> Be a racing car in a race.
> Be a leaf gently floating to the ground in the warm breeze.
> Be a boxer boxing in a boxing ring.
> Be a balloon floating in the air.
> Be a baby being rocked in a mother's arms.
> Be a stiff flagpole with your flag flying on the top.

5. Following the mimes discuss:
   Which mimes felt hard and stiff?
   Which mimes felt soft and gentle?
   Which mimes made you feel calm?
   Which mimes did not make you feel calm?

Guided Imagery

Ask students to find a comfortable spot and lie down and be very quiet. Read the following scenario.

It's a beautiful, warm, sunny day and you are at the beach. You put on your sunglasses **P** you put on your hat. You start putting on your sunscreen. While you are putting on your sunscreen you see a red boat with yellow sails. **P** You walk over and get in. You look up and see the breeze blowing gently in the sails. You can feel the warm breeze in your hair, on your face and on your body. It feels so wonderful. It even makes you feel sleepy. You decide you will take a nap. You drop your anchor, lie down and close your eyes. **P** You can feel your red boat rock gently in the waves.   While you are lying there, you hear the wind blow a little louder and you feel your little boat rock a little more. **P**   The wind starts to get stronger and the boat rocks more. **P**   The wind gets even stronger and the waves start to get bigger. You feel like your boat is inside a huge washing machine as you are thrown from side to side. **P** You hold on tight so that you don't fall out. **P**   Still the boat spins and rocks in the water. You hold on tighter and listen to the wind and the waves. **P** The wind howls and the waves crash on the side of the boat. **P**   While you are lying there the wind slowly starts to change. You feel the wind getting softer. **P**   Your boat starts to rock less violently. The wind gets softer and softer. **P** The waves start to get calmer and calmer and calmer. Your boat starts to rock gently in the water again. **P** You again feel the gentle breeze and the warm sun on your skin. Your boat rocks so gently and calmly that you feel calm too and you fall asleep. **P**

Procedure

1. Discuss the following:

    How did you feel when you first got in the boat?
    How did you feel when the wind started getting stronger?
    How did you feel when the waves were throwing your boat around in the waves and you nearly fell out?
    How did you feel when the wind and waves started to get weaker?
    How did you feel when the wind and waves were again soft and gentle and the warm sun was on your skin?
    Encourage students to use or introduce words such as:

Calm	Anxious	Relaxed
Worried	Peaceful	Frightened
In control	Scared	Out of control

2. Ask the children to think of all the words that mean the same as 'calm' and 'not calm'.

    Example:

Calm	Not calm
In control	Frightened
Peaceful	Worried
Relaxed	Out of control
Cool	Anxious
Good	Angry
Soft	Hot

3. Children fill in Worksheet 9 to reinforce feeling calm and feeling not calm.

Worksheet 9 Calm and Not Calm

Draw a picture of when you are calm and when you
are not calm.

Name:...

Write about your picture in the space next to it.

⟵ This is calm

_____

_____

_____

_____

_____

This is not calm ⟶

_____

_____

_____

_____

_____

Activity 15: Be Calm and Cool

Purpose
▶ to demonstrate how feeling out of control or anxious can interfere with people's ability to make decisions and solve problems

▶ to provide children with opportunities to learn about and practise strategies that will help them to calm down.

Resources
▶ an open space for drama activities
▶ Worksheet 10: 'Cool, Calm and In Control'
▶ a box of tissues.

Procedure
Some of the activities may be difficult for young children to perform. Alternatively ask another classroom teacher or older students to assist with modelling scenarios. After scenarios have been modelled, provide the children with an opportunity to try them out with partners.

1. Tell children that they are going to play more games that teach about being calm and why being calm can be good for you.
2. Revise what being calm means.
3. Ask the children to find a space in the room and show you the following:

Calm Face	Worried Face
Calm Face	Angry Face
Calm Hands	Frightened Hands
Calm Hands	Out of Control Hands
Calm Bodies	Worried Bodies
Calm Bodies	Out of Control Bodies
Calm Bodies	

4. Ask children which feels better and why.

Role Play

Ask children if an out of control body can fix problems.

Following responses, tell children they will do some experiments to see if out of control bodies can fix problems.

Choose a child to take part in a play with you in which they have lost their mother at the show. You will be another person who tries to help them. Tell the child they are not allowed to talk and they have to keep crying throughout the play.

During the role-play with the child, make comments that demonstrate how hard it is to hear what they are saying and find ways to help them.

Following the role-play ask the child:

How did your body feel?

How did your head feel?

Could you think clearly?

While you were upset, could you find a way to fix your problem?

Ask the other children what the child could do to feel better and try and fix their problem. Look for responses such as 'stop crying', 'calm down', 'relax'.

Ask the children how they might be able to calm down.

Show them and discuss Worksheet 10: 'Cool, Calm and In Control'. This Worksheet recommends making your body soft. To demonstrate this, conduct the following relaxation strategy:

Relaxation Strategy

Lie down on the floor

Push your arms out as long and hard as you can, then make them longer and harder.

Push so that your body and legs are as hard and long as you can

Push harder and harder.

Stop pushing.

Relax

Let go and make your body soft.

REPEAT

Replay the scene of the lost child but tell the students that this time after a while they must let you help them as you take them through the steps on Worksheet 10.

Scenarios

Choose other student and work through the following scenarios. Following each scenario ask the questions:

How did your body feel?
How did your head feel?
Could you think clearly?
While you were upset, could you find a way to fix your problem?

Then replay the scene using calming strategies.

Scenario 1:

Student's role   A student who has jammed their finger in a door and does not stop crying.

Teacher's role   Another student who tries to help.

Scenario 2:

Student's role   A student who is being stopped from playing on the play equipment by a bully. The student sits in a corner and won't speak to anyone.

Teacher's role   A teacher who tries to help.

Scenario 3:

Student's role   A student who is accidentally hit in the head with a football. They are very, very angry and want to fight. Tell them they can shout a lot and pretend to try and hit you.

Teacher's role   A friend who tries to help.

Provide the students with an opportunity to enact role-plays with partners.

Debrief

With any role-play activity it is important to fully discuss the performance and to separate students from the characters and the feelings they have experienced. This can usually be done by fully discussing each role-play with the students, discussing the feelings experienced and clarifying that all the players were acting.

Use questions like:

How are you feeling?
What are you thinking?
Have you ever experienced those feelings in other circumstances?
Are you back to your real self now?
Have you returned to the feelings you felt before the role-play?

Once students have had sufficient time to express their feelings, the teacher could offer words of encouragement and point out that the role-play was only make believe.

For example:

'That was very good acting.'
'We all know 'so and so' was only pretending.'

The role-play session is over when every student is back to being themselves.

Extension Activities

▶ Begin five minutes of quiet time after each lunch break for students to practise calming steps.
▶ Students invent their own calming games and plays to try with the class.
▶ Students ask their families what their best tricks for calming down are.

Name...

Cool, Calm and In Control

It's important to practise calming down.

If you are not calm, your body will not let you think.

If you can't think properly, you won't be able to work out a way to fix your problem.

Ways to calm down:

Take a few very deep breaths

Slowly count to five

Make your body soft

Wipe your tears away

Blow your nose

Have another deep breath

Think about ways to fix your problem

Make your body strong

Walk away until you feel calm

Think about 'happy' things

Then try to fix your problem!

Mistakes and Muck-ups

In this theme we explore what might go wrong to spoil a good time. Children also learn that they can fix and get over mistakes and muck-ups. 'It's a mucked-up moment, but I can fix it' is a slogan taught to children to assist them to think positively about difficult situations. Solutions for a range of age related problems are explored through the problems of nursery rhyme characters.

Activity 16: Mistakes and Muck-ups

Purpose

▸ to explore what might go wrong to spoil a good time

▸ to demonstrate that mistakes and muck-ups:

> are made by everyone
> are not permanent
> can be overcome
> provide opportunities to learn.

Resources

▸ a range of picture story books that feature characters that make mistakes

▸ two pieces of A3 paper, one headed, 'Mistakes and Muck-ups at Home', the other 'Mistakes and Muck-ups at School'

▸ Mistakes and Muck-ups, Posters 1, 2 and 3

▸ 'I Fixed a Mucked up Moment' Award

Procedure

For the purposes of this activity, the concepts of mistakes and muck-ups are very broad. Mistakes and muck-ups may refer to the things individuals can do that cause themselves or others to feel negatively. Muck-ups may also refer to instances in which a good time is spoiled; for example, when you get sick at a party, when another child breaks your toy or when someone is being mean to you.

1. Read a picture storybook that portrays a mistake or muck-up.
2. Discuss what a mistake or muck-up is.
3. Discuss mistakes made or muck-ups experienced by different characters in the book - how they felt, how they fixed up their mistakes and muck-ups and how they and other characters felt at the end of the story.
4. Ask students if they have ever made a mistake or muck-up. Ask for examples and how they felt at the time.
5. List examples on the 'Mistakes at Home' and 'Mistakes at School' posters.

6. Read through the lists. For each example ask:

> can this mistake be fixed?
>
> how can it be fixed?
>
> can we learn anything from the mistake?
>
> is it a mistake that will last for a short time or a long time?

7. Role-play some of the mistakes listed and ways they can be fixed.

8. Show and discuss:

> Mistakes and Muck-ups – Poster 1
>
> Mistakes and Muck-ups – Poster 2
>
> Mistakes and Muck-ups – Poster 3

9. Tell the students that if they make a mistake or experience a muck-up, they could say out loud,

> 'It's a mucked-up moment, but I can fix it!'

Think of what they can do to fix the problem. If they can't think of a way to fix the problem they can ask other people or an adult to help them.

10. Regularly present students with awards for identifying mucked up moments and attempting to fix them.

Extension Activities

▸ Personal or fictitious recounts

Students draw and write about their worst day ever or a fictitious character's worst day ever. (Please note it needs to be a scenario with a positive ending.)

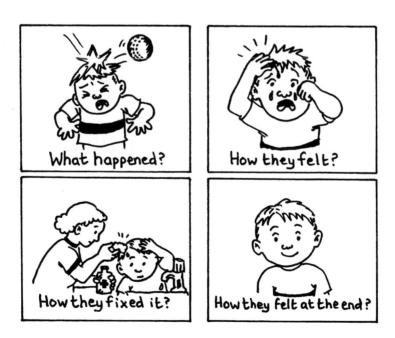

Mistakes and Muck-ups

Everyone makes them

They do not last for ever

Most of them can be fixed

Muck-ups help us to learn

Mistakes and Muck-ups–Poster 2

When I make a mistake or a muck-up happens,

I can choose to do nothing about it and feel bad,

Or

I can choose to fix it up and feel better!

It's a
mucked up moment

BUT

I CAN FIX IT!

'I Fixed a Mucked-up Moment '

Award

This award goes

to ....

for not letting a mucked-up moment
spoil a good time.

Well Done!

Activity 17: Nursery Rhymes

Purpose

▶ to provide students with practice at:

  identifying feelings and problems

  finding ways to solve problems.

Resources

▶ a range of nursery rhymes that depict mistakes and muck-ups. For
example:

  Old Mother Hubbard

  Jack and Jill

  Humpty Dumpty

Procedure

1. Ask students to recite a nursery rhyme.
2. Ask students to:

   Identify the mistakes or muck-ups in the rhyme

   Identify how the characters must have felt. Include associated characters
   such as Jack and Jill's mother.   Use Marvellous Masks as an aid.

   Recite the slogan introduced last session. 'It's a mucked-up moment but I
   can fix it.'

   Identify ways the mistake or muck-up can be fixed.
3. Discuss or enact role-plays in which there are resolutions to the problems.

Bunji

Children are introduced to Bunji, a rather shy character from another land that has come to join the class. The children have a lot to teach Bunji and Bunji has a lot to teach the children. The arrival of Bunji puts all of the children's new skills into action as they prepare to welcome Bunji and help Bunji settle into his new school. With the help of the children, Bunji is transformed into a bouncy, resilient and fun loving character that learns that it is better to seek help or to face your problems.

Activity 18: Bunji

Purpose

▸ to promote a welcoming, caring and supportive learning environment
▸ to reinforce concepts and strategies covered earlier in the unit
▸ to further explore concepts of similarities and difference between people
▸ to explore potential problems if people are classified by skin colour, birthplace, language, dress or diet.

Resources

▸ Bunji - A medium size, interesting looking soft toy that you feel will appeal to your children (Bunji does not make an appearance until the next session.)
▸ a photograph of Bunji
▸ Letter 1 from Bunji.

Procedure

If more than one class is implementing this programme, it is advised that each class choose a different name for their Bunji character.

1. Tell the students that you have received a letter from a person who wants to join the grade. Read the letter to the children. The letter can be used as a shared reading text.

2. Explain that:
> Bunji comes from another land.
> In this other land they speak differently and they do things differently.
> Bunji looks very different.

3. Discuss:
> Why Bunji is feeling nervous about coming.
> How they think Bunji will feel when he comes to school.
> Ways to help Bunji feel good about the new class.

4. Make a list of nice things the class can do to welcome Bunji. (Refer the students back to strategies suggested and the poster made in Activity 1.)

For example: ways to make Bunji feel welcome:
> Make a welcome sign
> Give him a drink and something to eat.
> Make a card.

Play games.

Smile.

Share toys.

Shake hands.

Draw some pictures.

Tell Bunji our names.

Show Bunji where the toilet is.

Find him a place to sit and a place to put his things.

Show Bunji around the school.

Get Bunji some books and pencils

Make sure Bunji has some company.

5. Discuss and list the things that Bunji will need to know. For example:

CLASSROOM RULES

➡ Always put your hand up to ask a question.

➡ Speak with a quiet voice.

➡ Put all rubbish into the bin.

PLAYGROUND RULES

➡ Keep the sandpit dry.

➡ Kick balls away from the buildings.

➡ Standing on top of the monkey bars is unsafe.

6. Go through the lists, discuss details with the children and allocate jobs.

7. Students draw pictures of Bunji's first day and how they can make him feel welcome.

Letter 1: A Letter From Bunji

Dear students,

My name is Bunji.

A little while ago I moved into the area and because I don't know anyone, I feel a bit lonely.

I heard this was a very nice school and that the people in this school look after each other. I would like it very much if I could join your class and make friends with everyone.

I must admit, I am a bit nervous because I have never been to school before. I come from another land where we look different and sometimes we do things differently.

I am sure that you will be able to teach me lots of things. I think I can also teach you things as well.

I am looking forward to our first day together and hope we can all be friends.

Yours with a hug and a kiss

Bunji

PS. I have included a photograph of myself.

Activity 19: Meeting Bunji

Purpose

▸ to reinforce welcoming strategies
▸ to reinforce calming strategies.

Resources

▸ Bunji (your soft toy)
▸ Letter 2 from Bunji
▸ Bunji's school bag, with a bag of lollies and a ball inside
▸ 'Cool, Calm and In Control' poster, Worksheet 10.

Procedure

1. Place Bunji in a place to hide, close to where children sit on the floor.
2. Tell students that Bunji finally came to school, however Bunji is very nervous and Bunji is not feeling calm at all. In fact Bunji is feeling out of control and Bunji is hiding.
3. Ask what can be done to help Bunji. Students will suggest a range of strategies.
4. Try some of them out but finish with going through the calming down strategies on the 'Cool, Calm and In Control' poster displayed in the classroom.

5. Tell the students that you heard Bunji wants to stop hiding.
6. Bring Bunji out to meet the children.
7. Read Letter 2 from Bunji, and look inside the bag.
8. Put all welcoming strategies organised by the students into place.
9. Play a game together using Bunji's ball.

Extension Activities

▸ Put Bunji on the class list.
▸ Establish a Bunji letterbox.
▸ Tell students that Bunji would love to get some letters from them.

Letter 2: A Letter From Bunji

Hi everyone,

Sorry I took so long to come out, but I didn't feel very calm at all. Thank you for helping me to be calm so that I could fix my problem and come out to meet you.

Already I am learning helpful things from you.

To show you that I want to be friends, I would like to share the lollies that my family packed for my play lunch.

I also have a new ball that you can play with if you like.

Hugs and kisses

Bunji

Activity 20: Bunji Blues

Purpose

▸ to reinforce welcoming strategies
▸ to reinforce calming strategies
▸ to reinforce the benefits of attempting to solve problems
▸ to enhance problem solving skills
▸ to promote optimistic thinking.

Resources

▸ Bunji
▸ Bunji's school bag containing Letter 3 from Bunji
▸ Worksheets 11 A, B and C: 'Bunji's got the Bunji Blues'. Paste one set of problems onto a sheet of paper for each child, enlarged to A3 if possible.

Procedure

1. Place Bunji and his school bag back in Bunji's hiding place while the students are out of the room.
2. Call the class register and call Bunji's name. Ask if anyone has seen Bunji and where he might be.
3. Ask some of the children to look in places were he might be - for example, in the toilet, in the head's office, in the toy box. Finally look in the cupboard.
4. Remark on how worried and sad Bunji looks.
5. Look in his bag and read the letter to the students.
6. Ask the children how they can help.
7. Go through the strategies on the 'Cool, Calm and In Control' poster.
8. Take Bunji out from hiding.
9. Ask the students to identify Bunji's problems.
10. Go through each problem and come up with suggestions to fix them.
11. Discuss possible consequences for suggestions given.
12. Ask the students to give the thumbs up sign for good suggestions and thumbs down sign for suggestions with bad consequences.
13. Tell Bunji to have a lie down and think about what to do to fix his problems.
14. Using prepared paper and Worksheets 11 A,B & C, students draw and write about what they would do if they were Bunji. Give each child one of the three. Make a class book entitled, 'Fixing The Bunji Blues'.
15. Prior to students leaving for the day, make mention of Bunji's problems and how you hope Bunji can fix them.

Letter 3: A Letter From Bunji

Dear Friends,

Sorry to worry you everyone, but I'm not having a very good day. When I got up this morning I was very hungry. I put my cereal into the bowl and added some sugar. Then I put a great big spoonful of my cereal in my mouth. Guess what? It tasted disgusting! Guess what else? I put salt onto my cereal instead of sugar. I spat it out and it went all over the table and into my grandmother's cup of tea. My grandmother asked what all the floaty bits were doing in her tea? I ran out of the room and started to cry.

 Then I went into the backyard to find my ball. Guess what? While I was looking for it, I knocked over a tin of paint. It went all over the grass. Then I got a box and put it over the paint so that my family wouldn't see it.

On the way to school, I was swinging my bag around and my lunch money fell out. I started to look for it but a big dog barked at me and it looked like it was going to jump the fence. So I ran away. Now I don't have any lunch money or any lunch. When I arrived at school I was so upset, I got in the cupboard.

Now I have a headache.

Hugs and tears

Bunji

Bunji's got the Bunji Blues

When Bunji got up this morning Bunji was very hungry. Bunji put his cereal into the bowl and added the sugar. Then Bunji ate a great big spoonful of cereal. It tasted disgusting. Bunji put salt on the cereal instead of sugar. Bunji spat it out and it went all over the table and into his grandmother's cup of tea. Bunji's grandmother came in and wanted to know what the floaty bits were doing in her tea. Bunji ran out of the room and started to cry.

If I was Bunji I would:

....

Bunji's got the Bunji Blues

Bunji went to find a ball in the backyard. While Bunji was looking for it, Bunji knocked over a tin of paint. It went all over the grass, so Bunji got a box and put it over the paint so that his family wouldn't see it.

If I was Bunji I would:

....

Bunji's got the Bunji Blues

On the way to school all the lunch money fell out of Bunji's schoolbag. Bunji didn't really mean to swing it so hard. When Bunji started to look for it a big dog barked and looked like it was going to jump the fence. So Bunji ran away. Now Bunji doesn't have any lunch money or any lunch.

If I was Bunji I would:

....

Activity 21: Bunji Bounces, Bunji Sings

Purpose

- ▶ to reinforce the benefits of solving problems
- ▶ to enhance problem solving skills
- ▶ to promote optimistic thinking.

Resources

- ▶ Bunji
- ▶ Bunji's school bag containing Letter 4 from Bunji and Bunji's poem
- ▶ Bunji's lifesaving elastic bungee jumping harness.

Procedure

You will need to make a harness from elastic. The bungee harness is to symbolize that Bunji is a resilient character that is able to bounce back after difficult times. This symbolism will help students identify with the concept. And provide the teacher with terms and images that can be used with the children.

1. Before the children come in, place Bunji in his bungee harness and attach him to something that will support his weight. (For added effect, decorate Bunji with flowers or something that shows that something good has happened to Bunji.)
2. When the children come in remark on how happy Bunji looks and ask why he is sitting in the elastic harness.
3. Bounce Bunji up and down in his harness.
4. Look in Bunji's bag and find and read Letter 4 followed by Bunji's poem.

Extension Activities

- ▶ Use Bunji's letter and poem as a shared reading task.
- ▶ Make his letter into a book for the children to illustrate and take home to read.

Letter 4: A Letter From Bunji

Dear Friends,

Thank you so much for helping me with my problems. I feel so wonderful I feel like I can fly. In fact, I can fly. Just watch me. I feel good because you taught me how to calm down and fix my problems.

Guess what? On the way home I walked near the place where the big angry dog lives. I saw the owner take it for a walk so I went and had a look for my lunch money. I found most of the money in the gutter. I put the money in my pocket and went home. I have also decided that from now on I will walk on the other side of the road so that the dog will not frighten me.

When I got home I ran into the kitchen. My Grandmother had just made a great big chocolate cake. She said to sit down and she gave me a great big slice with a glass of milk. She wasn't even angry any more. I said Grandma, sorry about spitting my cereal into your tea. She gave me another slice and said it didn't matter. When I finished the cake I made a sign for the salt dish that said, 'salt'. Grandma gave me a big wink and I went into the back yard.

I was hoping that the paint had gone away. But it hadn't. And there was dad. He looked cross. I walked over.

He said, 'How did this happen?'

I nearly said the dog knocked it over and then remembered we didn't have a dog. Martians, naughty goblins, and clumsy elephants all ran through my mind.

'Well'? said Dad.

I decided to be honest.

'Sorry Dad, I was looking for my ball and I knocked it over.'

Dad was not pleased.

'Why didn't you tell me? I needed that paint to finish painting the fence. Now the paint has dried all over the grass. Look at the mess. If you had told me I might have been able to clean it off.'

I felt very bad. Dad was just about to shout at me when I said, 'Dad you can have some money from my lunch to pay for some more paint'. I held out the money. Dad looked down at me and shook his head. Then we went to the garage to get the shovel. We dug up the grass with the paint on it and we planted some grass seed. We even put a little fence around the seed so that no one would step on it. I watered the grass seed carefully. Dad ran his fingers through my hair and said, 'Well done!'

Dad told me that it was my job to water the grass every few days.

Grandma stuck her head out of the back door and called out to Dad, 'I told you not to leave that paint out there'. She looked cross with Dad. Dad looked at me and winked.

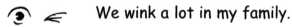 We wink a lot in my family.

Anyway. Thanks everyone. Without your help I'd still be in the cupboard. And if you sit in the cupboard you can't fix anything.

Hugs and kisses

Bunji

PS. I have written you a little poem that might help you if you have a problem to fix.

Bunji's poem
Bunji Bounces, Bunji Sings

Bunji Bounces
Bunji Sings
Bunji can fix,
Most things.

When something happens and he's out of control,
He calms down to rock and roll,
If he can't find an answer and he still feels blue,
He'll tell someone how he's feeling so they can help too.

Bunji Bounces
Bunji Sings
Bunji can fix,
Most things.

Chop down your problems
Chop! Chop! Chop!
Then you'll be able to
Skip and hop.

Snip down your problems
Snip! Snip! Snip!
Wouldn't you prefer to
Hop and skip?

Some problems are stubborn,
Some problems are tough,
Bunji learned to say enough,
Don't let your problems stay forever,
Let them go and shout I'm clever.

I'm clever!!!!!
Bunji Bounces
Bunji Sings
Bunji can fix,   SOFT
Most things.

Bunji Bounces
Bunji Sings
Bunji can fix,   LOUDER
Most things.

Bunji Bounces
Bunji Sings
Bunji can fix,   LOUDER
Most things.

Bunji Bounces
Bunji Sings
Bunji can fix,   LOUDER
Most things.

Bunji Bounces
Bunji Sings
Bunji can fix,   VERY LOUD
Most things.

Party Time!

By now children have much to celebrate. They have demonstrated what a caring and friendly class they are. A party is certainly in order. A good party needs to be planned and everyone has to help. Party preparations build a sense of belonging and teamwork as everyone works together for a common purpose.

A 'Happy Party Poster' is made to ensure everyone has a good time.

After the party, the class discusses whether the party was successful with positive party behaviour being rewarded. Books, poems, and artwork are created so that the party will be remembered.

Activity 22: Let's Have A Party

Purpose

▶ to demonstrate the importance and benefits of preparing for important occasions
▶ to build a sense of belonging and teamwork
▶ to enhance feelings of positive self regard
▶ to celebrate success.

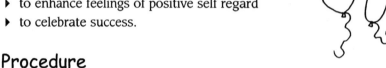

Procedure

Discussing and preparing for the party may take several sessions. It is suggested that you deal with one issue at a time and allocate roles or tasks. Much of the preparation can be linked into your language block. Links may include:

▶ making lists
▶ writing invitations
▶ following instructions for making a cake
▶ writing a timetable for the party etc.

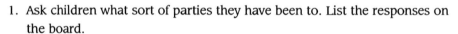

1. Ask children what sort of parties they have been to. List the responses on the board.
2. Ask students why they have parties. Discuss how all of these parties are to celebrate something special.
3. Suggest to the children that they are special and that the class is special. Ask them why they are special and what special things they have done during the term. List responses on the board. Provide some teacher responses that reinforce concepts delivered during the unit, for example:
   we treat people in our class nicely
   we welcome people to our class
   we share our things with people
   we showed Bunji how to solve his problems.
4. Admire the list of responses and say, 'Look at how special we are, why don't we have a party to celebrate our class'. Tell the children that good parties need to be planned and prepared for.
5. Ask the children what sort of party they would like. Ask children to sit in a circle and share their ideas with the class.
6. As a class, discuss and decide on the party details including:
   a place and a time to have the party
   the kind of party (Fairy, Monster etc.) and what to wear

invitations
food, decorations and games
music and songs
helpers
who will do and bring what
how to include Bunji.

Extension Activities

▸ Picture storybooks about parties.
▸ Give each child a large cardboard plate to decorate as a party cake. Provide a range of interesting and colourful odds and ends for the children to use such as sequins, pasta, wool, confetti etc.

The following recommendations will provide experiences that will promote a sense of belonging and positive self-regard.

Inviting parents to the party provides students with an opportunity to showcase their work and promote ideas presented in the unit. For example teachers could:

▸ Introduce Bunji to the parents and get students to explain who Bunji is and what Bunji has learnt
▸ Demonstrate role-plays in which students use calming strategies and problem solving ideas
▸ Ask students to recite the Bunji poem
▸ Ask students to sing songs related to the theme
▸ Have a welcome sign for parents
▸ Have a child formally welcome parents to the party
▸ Provide parents with tea and coffee and special parent party food.

Parents could also supervise games that are played. In that way you can create smaller groups and the students will get more of an opportunity to participate in activities. This will also help parents to feel comfortable and included.

▸ Involve children in making decorations and invitations.
▸ As a class make a cake for the party and decorate it together.
▸ Take photographs of the students involved in preparations.
▸ Make or bring a small gift to put in a gift box.
▸ Draw names out of a hat and give gifts.

Activity 23: A Good Party is A Happy Party

Purpose
▸ to identify positive social behaviour for group activities.

Resources
▸ Worksheets 12, 13 and 14

Procedure

1. Ask children what would make a party happy and what would make a party unhappy.
   Write responses onto sheets of paper under the following headings:
   'At a Happy Party.'
   'At an Unhappy Party.'

2. Cut responses into sentence strips. Jumble the sentences up. Ask students to reassemble the sentences under the correct headings.

Yummy		have	we	food	

quiet	have	to	we	very	be

3. Children complete worksheets 12,13 and 14.
   Instruct children to:
   ▸ read the sentences and colour in the happy or sad face.
   ▸ find all the happy party sentences and glue them under the happy party picture.
   ▸ find all the unhappy party sentences and place them under the unhappy party picture.
   Alternatively, ask children to draw a happy and unhappy party and glue the sentences to their artwork.

4. Ask the students to make sure this is a happy party for all children.
   The list of 'At A Happy Party' sentences can be used as a happy party checklist and as a tool to evaluate the success of the party.

   We eat yummy food   Everyone shares their toys
   Everyone helps clean up   Everyone plays together.

5. Make the 'At A Happy Party' check list into a poster. Decorate the poster in a party theme.

AT A HAPPY PARTY

Everyone eats yummy food.

Everyone plays together.

Everyone follows the rules of the games.

Everyone shares the toys.

Everyone speaks nicely to each other.

Everyone tries hard to make each other feel good.

Everyone helps to clean up.

Extension Ideas

▸ Make up the beginning of a story that tells about the worst party ever.
For example:

'The other day I went to a birthday party. It was no ordinary birthday party.
It was a terrible, horrible, no good birthday party. It was the worst birthday
party ever. When I got there I walked inside and guess what? The birthday
girl came up to me and snatched the present out of my hand. When she
opened it, she turned up her nose. I felt rotten. Then guess what happened
...I went to play with some people and someone told me to go away. Then
guess what happened (the children continue with the story).

Name:...

Happy Party, Unhappy Party

Read the sentences and colour in the happy or sad face.

Find all the happy party sentences and glue them under the happy party picture.

Find all the unhappy party sentences and place them under the unhappy party picture.

  Everyone plays together.

  Someone won't let other children play.

  Everyone has fun.

  Everyone shares the toys.

  Someone takes another child's cake.

  Everyone eats yummy food.

  Someone says rude and nasty words.

  Someone starts a fight.

  Everyone helps to clean up.

  Someone is greedy.

Name:..

At a Happy Party

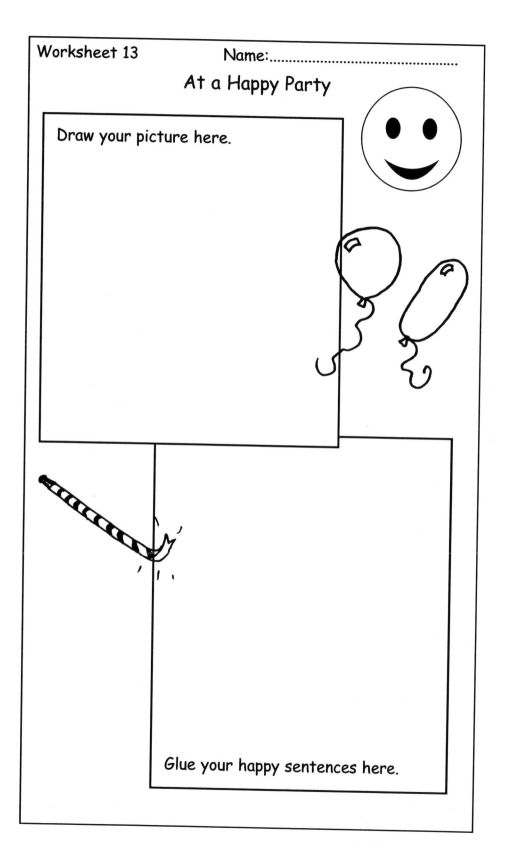

Draw your picture here.

Glue your happy sentences here.

Name:..

At an Unhappy Party

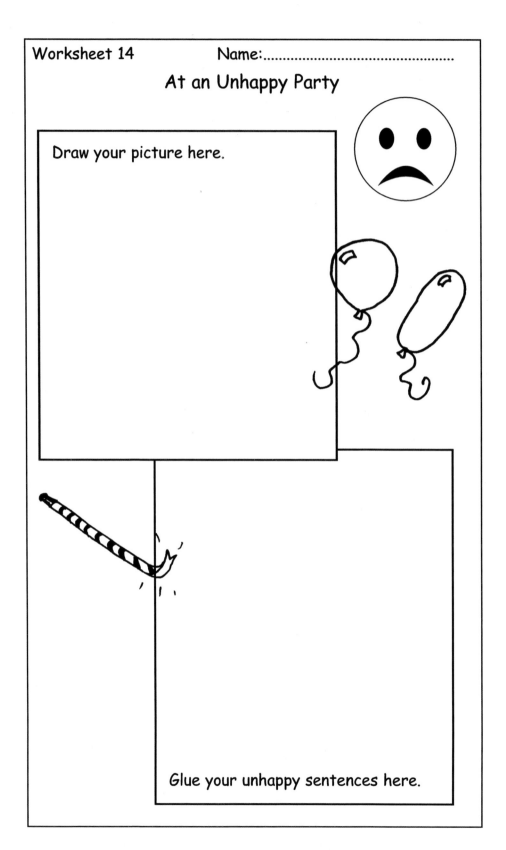

Draw your picture here.

Glue your unhappy sentences here.

THE HEART MASTERS

Activity 24: The Perfect Party

Purpose

▶ to provide a rich source of language experience opportunities
▶ to provide an opportunity for children to reflect on the party and identify:
    positives
    negatives
    ways of improving the party.

Resources

▶ 'Perfect Party Pal' Awards for each child
▶ some paper and crayons.

Procedure

If any mishaps took place during the party, work through the following:

▶ what went wrong?
▶ did the people involved use calming down strategies?
▶ how could things be done differently next time?

1. Engage the children in general discussion about the party.
2. Ask them to draw and write about their party work.
3. Bring the children back to discuss their work.
4. Refer back to the 'Good Party Check List' developed earlier.
5. Go through each of the points on the checklist and give them a big tick if they were achieved.
6. Congratulate the children for all their hard work in preparing for the party and for having wonderful party behaviour.
7. Present each child with a 'Perfect Party Pal' Award.

Perfect Party Pal Award

to

....

Bibliography

Adler, A (1943) *Understanding human nature*, London, Allen and Unwin.

Armstrong T (1999) *Seven Kinds of Smart: Identifying and developing your intelligences*, Plume, USA.

Benard, B (1991), in Growing Up In Australia: *The Role of Parents in Promoting Positive Adolescent Development*, (1999) Commonwealth Department of Family and Community Services, Australia.

Butler K (1997) 'The anatomy of resilience', *Family Therapy Networker*, March/April, 22-31.

Catalano R (1997) Promoting the potential of young people: *Communities that Care*, Paper presented in Melbourne, May.

Compas B, Hinden BR & Gerhardt CA (1995) 'Adolescent Development: Pathways of risk and resilience', *Annual Review of Psychology*, 46, 265-93.

Frydenberg, E. (1997) *Adolescent Coping Theoretical and Research Perspectives*, Routledge, New York.

Frydenberg, E. (editor) *Learning to Cope; Developing as a Person in Complex Societies*, 1999, Oxford university Press, UK

Fuller A (1998) *From Surviving to Thriving: Promoting Mental Health in Young People*, Australian Council for Educational Research, Melbourne.

Fuller, A., McGraw, K and Goodyear, M (1999) 'Bungy - Jumping Through Life: what young people say promotes well-being and resilience', *Australian Journal of Guidance and Counselling'*, 9 , 1, 159-168.

Gibson-Cline, J.; *Adolescence from Crisis to Coping: A Thirteen Nation Study*, Butterworth-Heineman Ltd, 1996

Goleman D, (1996), *Emotional Intelligence*, Bloomsbury, London.

Goleman D, (1998), *Working with Emotional Intelligence*, Bloomsbury, London.

Rayner M & Montague M (1999) *Resilient Children and Young People*, Deakin Human Services, Australia, Deakin University.

Resnick MD., Harris, LJ., & Blum RW, (1993), 'The impact of caring and connectedness on adolescent health and well-being', *Journal of Paediatrics and Child Health*, 29 (Suppl. 1), S3-S9.

Seligman M, Reivich K, Jaycox L, Gillham J, (1995), *The Optimistic Child*, Random House, Australia.

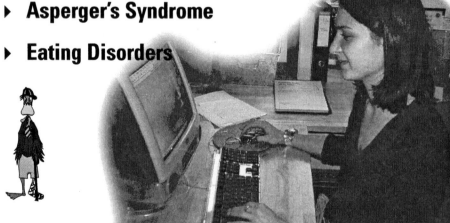